Some of the Most *Encouraging* Poems for You

Simple, Easy to Read
and
Memorize Inspirational Poems

Michelle Marie Richardson

WESTBOW
P R E S S®
A DIVISION OF THOMAS NELSON
& ZONDERVAN

WestBow Press books may be ordered through booksellers or by contacting:

WestBow Press
A Division of Thomas Nelson & Zondervan
1663 Liberty Drive
Bloomington, IN 47403
www.westbowpress.com
1 (866) 928-1240

Because of the dynamic nature of the Internet, any web addresses or links contained in this book may have changed since publication and may no longer be valid. The views expressed in this work are solely those of the author and do not necessarily reflect the views of the publisher, and the publisher hereby disclaims any responsibility for them.

Any people depicted in stock imagery provided by Getty Images are models, and such images are being used for illustrative purposes only. Certain stock imagery © Getty Images.

ISBN: 978-1-9736-2020-4 (sc)
ISBN: 978-1-9736-2019-8 (e)

Print information available on the last page.

WestBow Press rev. date: 07/09/2018

$\mathcal{C}$ontents

Introduction

Writing and reading Christ-centered and other positive writings has always been a way for me to cope and to become encouraged, inspired and uplifted in life. By the grace of God, it just comes naturally for me to write a poem based off of anything I may read, think of or feel. Therefore, I wrote these poems in order to help myself as well as others who are going through some of the same trials that I experience. In fact, during my worst trials, I have written the most poems. Some have been written years ago and others just recently.

No matter what brings this book or any of these poems across your path, I hope that you find just the right words at just the right time, as I did, in order to make your life better in the most positive ways.

This book is dedicated to all who seek God the Father and Jesus Christ, our Lord and Savior.

Life When You Beat Me Down

Life when you beat me down
Till my light skin turns black and brown
Till I feel spent and about to drop
Don't think you're gonna make me stop

Life when you hurl your stones
That make me shake inside my bones
And tear up deep inside my face
Don't think I'll stay inside that place

Life when you let others deal
Hate, betrayal, scars and steal
And try to make me lose my shine
Don't think I won't end up just fine

Life, I was made to always stand
And wiggle out of Satan's hand
If ever him I let me grip
And not to be a sinking ship

Those whom he sends to strike their blows
Because I am the Lord's he knows
I will outsmart and be protected
And their strikes are to them directed

I'll trust God with my life and breath
And fight and press and trod till death
And Jesus will perfect my soul
And give me thrice what Satan stole

Everything Will Be Alright

Everything will be alright
Things will work out for the best
The future will be very bright
You'll pass every single test

Everything will be alright
Things will go all well and good
There's no need to be uptight
That much should be understood

Everything will be alright
On this you can meditate
Yes, they will be not they might
Or else they will be good or great

Everything will be alright
Your head should be held up high
Your heart should always be light
You should never doubt or sigh

Everything will be alright
This attitude has to stick
Day by day, night by night
Through ups and down, thin and thick

Everything will be alright
Put it in your mind like glue
God has already won the fight
And that is how you'll make it through

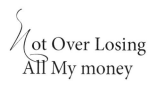ot Over Losing All My money

Not over losing all my money
Will I kill my own insides
Will I turn my back on Jesus
To where burning fire resides

Not over losing all my money
Will I let my love wax cold
Will I then resort to hatred
Not for things eyes can behold

Not over losing all my money
Will I choose to not commit
To the thing that I commit to
Love for others that won't quit

Because losing all my money
Must not drive me into hell
Many things they've taken from me
But still things have all worked out well

I will try to be a good steward
And to with it wisely deal
But I still will be alright
If some cheat, get over, steal

So the Lord always takes over
And restores all things to me
But I only have one soul
And that's worth more than my money

Every Day I Must Be Renewed

Every day I must be renewed
To the Lord I am glued
Troubles of the days gone
Are not to be concentrated on

Get up and have new plans
All the angels are my fans
God is my partner. God is my guide
Get fixed up and go outside

Make the calls I need to make
Take the time I need to take
Read the things I need to read
Do what I should do to succeed

Do what I may not feel like
Tell the devil to take a hike
When he tries to keep me in bed
And be ready to use my head

And constructively use my mind
Still leaving yesterday's worries behind
No past offenses being reviewed
Every day I must be renewed

Don't Cater to the Body, Cater to the Mind

Cater to the mind not body and
Things that are important you will understand
Things that are hard to reach you will find
Don't cater to the body, cater to the mind

Find a seed from Jesus from which to grow
Think of the things the mind would really like to know
About Jesus, yourself, others, things significant
Focus on the immediate environment

Picture the world as being sin free and clean
Understand God's words or find out what they mean
He will help you to communicate crystal clear
And say things sin free people like to hear

The mind is at its best when Christ is magnified
The body is at its best when in a way it has died
For the body has taken lots of abuse
Yet the mind can help all to overcome and goods produce

Cater to peoples' interests, hearts and needs
Every chance you get, plant some Jesus seeds
Leave the flesh and the body and its sins behind
Don't cater to the body, cater to the mind

$\mathcal{S}$peak God's Will into Being

Speak God's will into being
Make it God you're seeing
Bring Jesus out among you
Whomever it is that you talk to

When you get nervous exhale
Open the Lord up like mail
That sends a message saying
From Him your mind is not straying

A word can have such power
When Christ is the endower
And words in His direction
Have His divine protection

Be kind in conversation
Be Christ's representation
His Holy Spirit is freeing
So speak God's will into being

H is Protection

Don't Worry About losing
It's Jesus you are choosing
He never has failed
Your ship hasn't sailed

You'll find your gain
Not down the drain
But right in front
Just what you want

Don't let the past
Cause you to lose
The future that
You need to choose

Choose to follow the Lord
His voice, His direction
Because you can't afford
To lose His protection

It's Time

It's time to stop reading and start doing
To stop staying and start going
To start moving and stop stagnating
To go on ahead and stop hesitating

It's time to do what you can and must
To let God be the One to trust
To act on faith and have a vision
To make a move after making the decision

It's time to let things fall into place
To meet responsibility face to face
To be a good steward and manage affairs
To let the One guide you that knows all your hairs

It's time to actively seek and find
To fully activate the mind
To use and organize a plan
To prove to others, "Yes, you can!"

It's time to let it not be you
But God who shows what you can do
But God whose face through you does shine
Yes, I'd say it's about that time

Take the Step

Things can go wrong, fall apart
You could be left high and dry
End up homeless or with a broken heart
Find you only want to cry

Things went wrong before but God got you through
Now just what are you going to do?
Close yourself up and take no chances
Hold down no job and forsake all romances?

Things can go right, the time could be near
You could remain faithful with joy and no tear
You could keep working, prosper greatly
Haven't you trusted in Jesus Christ lately?

Thinking ahead to the next decades
You could be singing, "My joy never fades"
As things turn out good and new and their best
Have faith. Take the step and let God do the rest

Imperfections

Imperfections plus care
God would never leave you bare
God would never leave you at all
He'll even lift you if you fall

No matter what happens, just relax
God will help you to the max
He has unlimited resources
No one outdoes His forces

His Son, Jesus has a mission
To keep you in a good condition
So, don't give in to bad feelings
Keep tons of joy that outreaches ceilings

And don't worry about imperfections
God's in the business of making corrections
You are His artwork and your life He'll mold
Despite all imperfections, you He does hold

This Happened for God's Glory, Dear

This happened for God's glory, dear
A blessing is so very near
God's blessing nobody can block
Just seek and seek and knock and knock

When things go down that seem amiss
There's something else, I'll tell you this
There's a plan God has unique
The future isn't bleak

There's something you don't understand
Defeat is not what God has planned
For you in life, but what He'll send
Is a beginning, not and end

Just picture what good God can bring
More than you ask and everything
Lift yourself up, then prepare
God's kindness isn't ever rare

God soon will let His favor show
If you did not know, now you know
If you did not hear, now you hear
This happened for God's glory, dear

You Are Validated

You have gone through a lot
But gone now you are not
Gone through you have for sure
You know you can endure

You are legitimate
You have so much good to get
On this earth where you dwell
So all doubt do dispel

Decisions that you make
Don't need a double take
With God's plans in mind
You won't be in a bind

You do the best that you can do
You speak as well as you can too
Now stick to what God gives
Around strangers, friends, enemies and relatives

Embrace how new you are
Because you've come so far
It has been demonstrated
That you are validated

Serve Him like Salt with Flavor

Relax with God wherever you are
Have a pure heart that none can mar
Remember Jesus with your speech
And all his power remains in reach

Start keeping Christ in your heart near
Dwell on His power, not your fear
Think of Christ in all your affairs
When among persons, groups and pairs

Don't sit there mind straying, sinking
When you could be of Jesus thinking
When you could be like light and shine
Saying to others, "Christ is mine"

So, sometimes style is not your hype
And sometimes you are not their type
You'll be the one with Jesus' favor
If you serve Him like salt with flavor

Think

Think on the moment
Think on your gifts
Think on your blessings
Forget your rifts

Forgive your enemies
Pray for your foes
Erase their offenses
Endure through the woes

Forget your shortcomings
Forget about flaws
Cling to Christ's salvation
Keep all of His laws

Think yourself forgiving
Think yourself at peace
Think yourself a child of God
Think, and don't cease

In Full

Stop thinking about who God isn't favoring
Stop thinking about troubles with faith wavering
Stop going up and down, down and up
Eat from My body, drink from My cup

Stop giving your power to some dark enemy
Trade in all your worries for full trust in Me
Resist all temptations and be secure
Obey My commands and your thoughts will be pure

Start remembering verses that shouldn't slip away
Security means renewal each day
Don't let lessons of warfare be given in vain
Seek, and you shall find answers again and again

Don't fuss over the things that matter less
Come out of the cold into My warm caress
I love you no matter what, please understand
God will let no one take you from out of My hand

Start knowing just where to go and what to do
Start knowing that God is taking care of you
Start obeying My words despite the world's pull
And let Me live in you since you're God's child in full

Humble, Faithful, Confident

Day by day, needs met
God's promise He won't forget
With who you are, God is pleased
Worries absent. Mind now eased

Step by step in confidence
Love of Jesus so intense
That faith expands to such degrees
That any opposition flees

In the heart the songs awake
Joy that nobody can take
Joy that nothing can destroy
Endless confidence and joy

One which no one can condemn
Loved more than a precious gem
God destined and God sent
Be humble, faithful, confident

God Gave Me a New Name

God gave me a new name
It's written within
Whatever I go through
I'm going to win

However things happen
I'm going to soar
To get the victory
Blessings galore

I am no longer
Identified
By the things of the past
That I wanted to hide

My new name is Victor
My new name is Winner
Not marred or banned
Or punished, lost sinner

I'll get a new place
And there I will stay
Just where Jesus is
With my new name, each day

Choosing Faith Not Fear

Choosing faith not fear
I give God my best
As His Word I hear
As by Him I am blest

I must move, not stall
Not waste the mind
Go along standing tall
Helping and acting kind

I must use the anointing
And feel the fire
And walk behind words pointing
To what will inspire

I must with the Lord view
Things in a special light
Just as I right now do
So that I will do right

Choosing faith not fear
This will not be, I trust
More than what I can bear
For obey God I must

Jesus is So Beautiful

Jesus is so beautiful
No one can deny
He can make me perfect
He dwells on high

Jesus is so beautiful
Anyone can see
He can produce a minister
Even out of me

Jesus is so beautiful
He can fix anything
He can make me joyful always
And cause my heart to sing

Jesus is so beautiful
He freely gives
Because He's so loving
And He endlessly lives

Jesus is so beautiful
He makes me content
Jesus is my Savior
Jesus is God sent

In Between

I'm in between comfort and a challenge
In between resting and restoration
In between recollecting and reorganizing
In between on and off of vacation

I'm in between nothing and something
In between few and a lot
In between weakened and strengthened
In between a have and a have not

I'm in between closed and blossomed
In between winter and spring
In between rain and sunshine
In between nothing and everything

So, I can let God do His work on me
Make my heart pure and my hands clean
Wait on Him while He makes all things ready
In the meantime, I'm in between

In God's Hand

God has you in His hand
Things might not go as planned
But you'll survive for sure
And yes, you can endure

God lifts you to your feet
He'll make your life complete
All that's bad He'll remove
He'll help you to improve

God keeps you calm and kind
So discipline your mind
Make Him your every thought
Then all Battles are fought

To win not lose or trip
To not let your foot slip
Obeying each command
God has you in His hand

All Around the Clock

I am satisfied
I am not denied
Things are truly progressing
There is a stay on God's blessing

Things are going that should be leaving
Things are coming that I should be receiving
It's a state of mind
I'm leaving the darkness behind

There are no jittery shakes
There are no funny flakes
There's no worry or fret
All that I can forget

Things that hinder are lost
Now there is joy at no cost
And such peace that fulfills
That the soul all of this thrills

Jesus heals and cures
Goodness He ensures
He is my Solid Rock
All around the clock

ever Go Back

Never go back
Leave the old behind
You are a whole new being
With a renewing mind

Always look forward
Know yourself well
Step ahead and move on
God loves you, you can tell

Never go back
To being afraid and unsure
To cracking under pressure
Or to worry impure

You can step out
Having faith to perform
Great things for the Lord
Since you've weathered each storm

Never go back
Find rest now on
For Jesus is the One
That you can rest upon

Let go of all the baggage
That once threw you off track
As you grasp all the Lord's mercy
And never go back

If God Gives it to Me, I Can Do It

If God gives it to me, I can do it
If He gives instruction I'll put my mind to it
It will be successful, that is true
I can do whatever God gives me to do

If God puts it in my heart I can
It's all a part of God's great plan
To get me to fulfill my calling
I will also be walking though now I am crawling

If God lets doors open I can go through them
The things I'm supposed to do, I can do them
Whatever the challenges and the tasks
For each one does receive who sincerely asks

When God sees me seeking and trying
It is on just Him that I am relying
And Jesus will equip me well
And the Lord will be with me. This I can tell

So, I must do and not hold back
And fast and pray and stay on track
And get on up and do my best
For surely God will do the rest

When You Say You Can't Cope

What do you mean when you say you can't cope?
God promises you a future and hope
Stop listening to the devil and lies
That your weaknesses say when with God you can rise

What do you mean when you say they won't arrive?
The things of your dreams that are why you're alive?
The things that you want to accomplish, obtain?
I do not want to hear you talk that way again!

What do you mean when discouragement binds
Your soul and your body to fears of all kinds?
Don't you know of God's power? It's Him you must seek
So, just turn to Him and then no more negatives speak

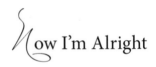ow I'm Alright

Now I'm alright once I check
My mind used to be such a wreck
My mind used to be in a toss
But now I'm carrying my cross

Now I'm alright, no longer sickly
I called on God. He helped me quickly
And now I seek and gladly find
I'm well in body, soul and mind

Now I'm alright. I'm not destroyed
And now my life is being enjoyed
I work and rest and carry on
Because I've Christ to rest upon

Now I'm alright. Things I couldn't fix
Took place when I was in the mix
But now I'm peaceful, sound and wise
Christ even opened up my eyes

Now I'm alright, calm, alert
My scars tell of past pain and hurt
Because of God's grace, I'm still here
Awake, alive and of good cheer

I leave the past and keep the now
I know the who the what and how
I've got the Way, the Truth the Life and the Light
And praise the Lord, now I'm alright

Purified Mind

Purified mind in spite of the beast
Purified love for even the least
Purified service for Jesus in heart
Within, with everyone doing our part

Purified mind in spite of worldly cares
Purified actions without panic flares
Purified thoughts that are calm and upright
On what is good and loving and light

Purified mind that can always face
The fact that it's purified by God's grace
Being freed by truth from death and sin
Being given God's love to wallow in

Purified mind in spite of whom
Is in my surroundings or in the room
I don't look at images but at the Lord
And how we will be praising Him in one accord

Purified mind that puts me at rest
God purified me, at my request
The enemy cannot defile or stay
Because God purified and renews me each day

God Clothed My Soul

God clothed my soul with special things
That keep me in all of my ways
That peace and joy and loving brings
That stay with me all of my days

God makes the future clear and bright
No matter what or who's around
He always is my source of light
He is the solution that's always found

There is no need for problems to lure
There is no need for worry or tension
God is there always, always the cure
There is no need to stay in suspension

God offers warmth. Just think on this
God is all comfort. He's in control
He's all we need. The world is His
And I thank God He clothed my soul

The Lord of All Peace

The Lord of all peace
Gives me peace by all means
And He holds all the keys
To the most sought for things

He meets and exceeds
All that I can expect
And provides all my needs
And He'll guide and protect

God keeps me intact
When chaos surrounds
And His love is a fact
And His mercy astounds

Because He is so great
The Lord answers prayers
And on Him I wait
And cast all of my cares

Crying

I'm crying to you
That's all I can do
I put my head down low
The tears just flow
The words I cannot speak
My heart feels so weak
Its flutters are so quick
My stomach feels sick
No other can comfort
I can't tell them I'm hurt
My mouth I must just close
And go to You who knows
No other delivers
My bubbling skin shivers
My chest lifts and caves in
It's "Dear Lord, Amen"
My hands are a face mask
"Please help me now" they ask
I lower each elbow
And then sway to and fro
I sit down and I kneel
Such discomfort I feel
My chin nearly hits my chest
Please, Lord put my mind to rest
Faith enters like the wind
My crying can now end
And once more I can stand
Since God, it's in Your hand

The Purpose, the Ache

The purpose, the ache
To serve is what it will take
To become fulfilled is the cure
To keep the whole heart pure

So empty and so in pain
The days so dull and plain
Nights restless, days cloudy
Shouts laziness loudly

It seems like a trap not a choice
Daily excuses tune out the voice
But nothing else soothes the ache
Serving the Lord is what it will take

God will stop the shutting of the eyes
God will stop the turning and the cries
If you opt to take the fearless route
And realize Christ will work it out

It's why you're present, why you're here
It's what without your heart cannot bear
Can't choose the trap. Don't want to die
The purpose and the ache is why

Give God the Glory

I owe it to God
It isn't my doing
All that I get done
All that I have brewing
Events in my life
Ways I've overcome
How far I have gotten
Where I have come from
I thank God for life
For every success
For I fall short so often
He provides nonetheless
On my own I am nothing
With Him I am strong
So, I give God the glory
All the day long
If I feel weak or weary
Or down or faint
He'll renew my strength quickly
No cause for complaint
I'll have faith in God
For as long as I live
And it is to Him only
The glory I give

Grace

I strive to follow God's commands
But when I fail, I pray for grace
And put it all in Jesus' hands
Who shed His blood to take sin's place

If I let guilt and shame invade
And make me feel I cannot serve
I waste the me that Jesus made
I lose my worth and lose my nerve

I judge myself when I should not
When all I must do is repent
And let go of the guilt I got
Since sinning isn't my intent

So from now on, I realize
That I can serve and do my part
Receive God's mercy and be wise
Since I was of a contrite heart

Grateful

I have Jesus, so I grow
I can make it, this I know
No matter what happens, anything
Inside my heart, I will always sing

Jesus has helped me to such an extent
So much harm against me He did prevent
So grateful I am that He made me His friend
And I know that His love for me will never end

There is power with Jesus that I now possess
It's what gets me through tough times, through struggles and stress
It's what keeps my spirit so strong and secure
Since it's His Spirit in me that helps me endure

That's because God is so good, with all of His might
That He sent us His Son who did everything right
I'll enjoy this great blessing as Jesus intended
And His love is so great it can't be comprehended

Faith Decides

Even more than I can ask
Covering every need
Mercy no one can mask
A Father, indeed

In spite of weak spots
In spite of lose holds
Never any have nots
Or out in the colds

Even if there were losses
If there were let goes
There would be no tosses
Of God-glory shows

But the promise sticks tightly
And God is not slack
It is not taken lightly
And not taken back

God gives new blessings each day
God fully provides
God will always be my stay
That's what faith decides

I Am Cured

Let the heavens now resound
Praise the Lord from all around
For of the affliction that once lured
I am cured

Let the victory bell ring
Let the heavenly angels sing
Those that ministered to my soul
With Christ have reached the winning goal

Now I strut on down the aisle
It's been a struggle and taken a while
But I can stand, feel strong and speak
Without the hold of havoc's wreak

On testifying I am bent
I've been given blessings that none could prevent
I now seek and find and face life's turns
But in me victory's fire now burns

Let the Lord be thanked and praised
Let the devil be amazed
God now reigns in my soul concretely
And Christ has won me over completely

From Jesus nothing can separate me
Not trial temptation or those who hate me
Not what I must face or what must be endured
Praise the Lord God almighty. I am cured

You Can Improve

You can improve and your life is worth living
You can learn how to love again and be forgiving
You can learn how to do the right things and to pray
And to let your heart match the things you do and say

That relay compassion and are very kind
You can let your actions match your mind
And your mind can be like Jesus' who rightly teaches
And the people you reach be the people He reaches

When you see your reflection, don't frown just smile
You will overcome struggles after a while
After turning to God who makes everything smooth
Yes, your life is worth living and you can improve

$\mathcal{B}$e a Witness

What discourages you from being a witness?
For the Lord God is with you even in this
Attack from the devil who Christ has defeated
Why not proclaim God's praises, said once then repeated

God is teaching you that your power is null
Without Him you are empty and with Him you're full
Of possibilities and potential
To do the Lord's will with the faith that's essential

Nothing can hold you down if you acknowledge
It's not about titles or smartness or college
It's all about grace which God gives you to steer
In the proper direction since God's always there

Humble yourself and let God do the pointing
Never forget that it is His anointing
Never think it depends on just you alone
But tell others about Jesus, the Cornerstone

Whatever you do, keep God first and pray
As you press through the path and try finding your way
Don't hate the lesson and make things quite hard
Tell of Christ your supplier whose blessings aren't barred

Forward Marching

Forward marching always means
Things get messy but God cleans
Maybe some can see you sweat
But that's okay. Don't give up yet

Onward moving, stomp and press
What some see is strain and stress
What God sees is a soldier, His
Proud of you? You bet He is!

Don't stop, drop and over roll
Despite the fire in your soul
Let it burn with every turn
The power of God you will learn

Do not give up, do not tire
Keep the passion and desire
To keep on marching to the tune
And you will reach fulfillment soon

Who I Call

Whom when I fall down do I call?
And whom do I upon depend
When I feel sure I'll lose it all?
God up above and Christ my Friend

And when I'm all alone and cold
And feel for sure that that's the worst
And feel discouraged, not so bold
I call upon the last and first

And when discomfort covers skin
And I feel hurt beyond repair
And when nobody lets me in
I call on God who's always near

And so I can with faith proceed
With whatever minute I've got
And God will supply every need
I'll call on God, even if not

He'll Make It Turn Out Right, No Doubt

Thank God although I know I'm low
Thank God for how the wind will blow
I can't predict but can be strict
All good will be the last verdict

Thank God, though me He didn't brief
On the forecast, yet there's no grief
I know that I don't need to worry
For He is the lawyer, the judge and the jury

Thank God for what's already fact
Though no announcement is exact
Until He makes it all pan out
He'll make it turn out right, no doubt

$\mathcal{I}$ Need a Way

I need a way to make it through
Lord, tell me please what I must do
Lord, give me purpose and a hope
When I view dreams and reply, "Nope,

I can't do this, I'm not equipped"
My confidence has now been stripped
Due to the label and the past
Lord, rescue me and show up fast

It's not the worst encountered dread
I'm still alive. I'm still not dead
Within my spirit, yet I kneel
And ask you, Lord to save and heal

Then I will always stop and turn
To You who makes the fire burn
Inside my heart, which makes me move
And prosper, do right and improve

I'm feeling low and friends are far
I never will believe You are
I'm asking, begging you today
Lord, get me through. I need a way

God is Good

God is good. That's what I know
Therefore, forward I just go
He makes the way and does direct
Things go better than I expect

God is good. I know it's true
It's Him that makes all that I do
Come out alright, despite that I'm weak
It's Him that day and night I seek

God is good and that's a fact
No matter how others act
No matter what enemies plan
His ways are not the ways of man

God is good and that won't change
Some circumstances may seem strange
When His path and His way we choose
But God makes it good and that's the good news

I'll Never Leave You
Nor Forsake You

I'll never leave you nor forsake you
This should very happy make you
You've even seen this in the past
I am the first. The first and last

I am sufficient to sustain you
In my mansion I'll contain you
When you think ways I can't make
But you I won't leave nor forsake

I love you and I will provide
All that you need on the inside
All in this world you'll ever need
I'll be right there with you, indeed

Put all your troubles in My hands
I am the One who understands
I'll cover flaws and each mistake, too
I'll never leave you nor forsake you

Through Jesus Christ Who Strengthens Me

Through Jesus Christ who strengthens me
I can be all I'm meant to be
I can do all things that I must
When Jesus Christ has all my trust

Jesus can take over it all
Whenever I may seem to fall
If I put all my trust in Him
Not in the things that appear grim

Through Jesus who strengthens me
I can a better future see
And walk on through a trial knowing
That Jesus' strength is in me growing

I can see sunshine when there's clouds
I can speak praise to God aloud
I can rest and be filled with glee
Through Jesus Christ who strengthens me

God Thoughts All Day Long

God thoughts all day long
Make it into a song
Praise Him, up on high
Anyone can, even I

God thoughts all day long
Nothing really can go wrong
That isn't corrected, sometimes slowly
He even perfects the lowly

God thoughts all day long
He seeks to make the weak strong
When the weak seek to give Him praise
He lifts them all up to others amaze

God thoughts all day long
What better company to be among?
God thoughts inspire and God thoughts heal
When God thoughts are thought of you know God is real!

Go Forward

Don't go backwards. Forward go
Where things clearly flow
Even when the pressures hit
Don't go backwards. Don't forget

God has raised you out of past
Scenes, disasters, troubles vast
That were not the places to trod
Don't go backwards. Look to God

When the troubles seem to come
Know what God has brought you from
And with Jesus sup and dine
Soon things will all turn out fine

Backwards many setbacks lie
Don't give up and do not die
Leave the imps and don't return
To the ones who'll only burn

Keep your future pathway straight
And repent before too late
If you slip and backwards sway
Decide to go forward each day

Found Love

Found love and I know that I'll make it
Found true love and nobody can take it
Found true love. Now I've blossomed and grown up
The love of my life has already shown up

Found everlasting love. I'm not insecure now
Found everlasting love. I'm glowing and pure now
Found everlasting love and it just goes on
Other things end but the love I found goes on

Found real love and rainbows remind me
Found real love and its trust and truth bind me
Found real love. I'm projecting the shines of it
Real love is special and so are the signs of it

Look at my eyes and you'll surely see love
Look at my smile. Yes, it has to be love
I feel uplifted, gifted, new also
And this can happen to you, also

God reached down and showed me this
He never had to or owed me this
What I thought was so special and so good
Compared to the love of God is just no good

True, everlasting love: Jesus Christ died for us
Real love: He pushed all life's pleasures aside for us
Seems like my life now revolves around love
Glory to God for I've finally found love

God Will Surely Bring the Blessing

People can't block anything
Make that make you want to sing
Do not worry. Do not cry
At any time when people try

To make things out of your reach
But be positive in self-speech
God gives solutions when you seek
Not let those people make you weak

So, be so strong when solutions hide
Let God, not foes be your guide
And keep the faith and keep pressing
God will surely bring the blessing

He's All You Need

God is who you have to choose
If everything or things you loose
What folk think is to be ignored
For within in you God is stored

Nothing can take Him away
At any time or any day
And having nothing also can't
True treasures within God will grant

As long as you have God in mind
There is no trial of any kind
That can destroy you. You'll succeed
He's all you've got. He's all you need

Undying Love

God, let me have undying love
Let Jesus be who I think of
And not the hatred that destroys
Lord, please return to me my joys

God let me not go down with hate
On You I call. For you I wait
My definition has to be
A cup of love. So help me see

Your light and love and easy yoke
With memories of what you spoke
To all who hear and have ears
And God, please remove all my fears

Lord, let it be that You are pleased
Even when my mind isn't eased
When serving You, Lord up above
God let me have undying love

It's Morning

It's morning and time to declare
That things aren't just up in the air
That things aren't as bad as they seem
It's time to say, "I have a dream"

Of smoothly going through the day
Of God making a lovely way
Of being able to cope well
Of having all good things to tell

And it is time to know it's true
Not to doubt and sadness turn to
But to a future nicely sent
With every moment that is spent

It isn't time to look and see
The tactics of the enemy
And want to hide or want to cry
But to succeed. Succeed and try

To obey God who wants you still
To be happy and in His will
Abide all times and everywhere
It's morning and time to declare

Comfort and Ease

Comfort and ease are not
The things to always get
But it is better if you've got
A strong mind that is set

Comfort and ease are sometimes wrong
They are not the things to seek
And you really must be strong
Strength keeps you from being weak

Comfort and ease throw out
Feel some discomfort and do
All the things you think about
That lack ease and discomfort you

Comfort and ease push away
When you lie inside your bed
And it is time to start your day
And think of life, not being dead

Life's worth isn't based upon
All the comfort you can find
Or all the ease that soon is gone
Put Jesus' power in your mind

Enjoy Now

Enjoy this moment. Enjoy now
Stand up tall and take a bow
All things best to be the plan
Done, projected, close the can

Into which you store the past
Put the cover on it fast
Now think of what this will bring
Present times and nice thinking

Thinking of your qualities
Discipline, peace, calm that frees
Thought that solves. A face that glows
A mind that teaches till it knows

Love for passing and surrounding
Happiness and hope abounding
That can't end and must continue
Keep those good attributes in you

When things seem a bit down dipped
Do not let your heart be ripped
Love more. Hope more. Seek and find
That same enjoyment, stand tall mind

ord, Keep Me

Lord, I love you. Do not take me
I can be whatever you make me
I can think however you desire
And always rise a level higher

Lord, keep me living and doing
Things that each day are renewing
Don't let me fall backwards, blinded
Of Your goodness keep me reminded

Lord, don't from me be depleted
That way I won't be defeated
Carry me when I can't rise
And free me of depression's lies

Lord, take over me and let me
Remember that you always met me
At my lowest and my highest
Things to encounter and to digest

Lord, please be my food and drink
I'll think what I'm supposed to think
And be assured of all your care
Lord, let me have a faith that's rare

God Gave Back

God brought me out of their traps
My obedience had gaps
But I ask God to forgive
And to not let me die but live

Surely foes can strike and vex
It all seems to be so complex
It all seems to be simple, too
Do not let foes take over you

That's what God simply commands
But I fell into their hands
Ignorantly. What a mess
But to God, my sin I confess

Now I'm getting one more chance
To do things that do enhance
Not destroy and not subtract
Avoid the foes, to be exact

Thank You God for mercy shown
Clearly, it's not on my own
That I got strong and back on track
You give me all that I lost back

Confidence and Faith

Confidence and faith-filled, guide
Me around not stuck inside
Me, Dear Father God, I pray
Every single God sent day

Confidence and faith-filled, lead
Me to what I want and need
Father God, I ask right now
And when I don't know show me how

Confident and faith-filled, face
Everything in every place
Well guided and all alright
Lord, make my days be very bright

Let Me Serve You

Let me serve you, please
Let me be at ease
Doing things that aide
In curing others that are sick and afraid

Let me get up everyday
And always find my way
To where I use my hands and feet
For Your work to be done and for your goals to meet

Lord, thank you for finding swift
Ways for me to serve, uplift
Myself and others, as You desire
And do the things that You require

God Can

God can do the impossible, truly
Take you to places you never thought you'd be
Get you through things that you used to dread
Put life inside of you so you won't be dead

God can make ways out of no ways
Make testimonies that invoke His praise
Keep you moving and get you going
Even when you don't know what God is doing

God can surely shape you and mold you
Even if sometimes He has to scold you
And Jesus makes everything all good and well
The impossible God can do. Now you can tell

God is Enough

What is in me as my guide
Is God buried deep inside
Which is my hope and my stay
No matter what, I'll be okay

Enemies and foes may rise
But it silences my cries
When I think of what's within
Instead of crying, I can grin

Every day when I awake and I
Think of God inside of my
Being, I can be fine
None can steal Him. He is mine

Things will all turn out just right
Even when it's faith, not sight
Even when times are very tough
If I have God in me then I have enough

Love Yourself

Love yourself is a command
When you've fallen. When you stand
God has all you'll ever need
To move on and then to succeed

Love yourself and all God is
To everyone who is His
To everyone, even those
That when He knocks, their doors they close

Love yourself and overcome
All obstacles, not just some
To God's presence showing
You right places to be going

Love yourself. Make no excuse
There's always something you can use
As evidence that God is great
So, love yourself before too late

God Is the One

God is the One who does all things
Amazing. Open doors He brings
He does it all once we turn knobs
Provides with shelter, finance, jobs

God is so eager to brightly shine
The credit is all His, not mine
I walk below a cloud of shade
And step into the ways He's made

God sets things up to make it known
He is so great. The world's His own
He wants to give abundant treats
Pathways paved with golden streets

I know God is this way because
He covers me despite my flaws
He'll keep me covered, by and by
I want to praise His name on high

Don't Feel Bad

Don't feel bad about ones who
You think have done things to you
Let it go and ride by
God is working. That is why

Don't take it into your mind
Leave it, leave it all behind
Keep your righteousness and yet
Free of bitterness do get

When you dwell on things done
By one and another one
Think of those who do come through
Despite what others did to you

Keep Encouragement

Keep encouragement hidden inside
Then your hands are open wide
To receive God's very best
And God will always do the rest

Keep thinking on what is right
And make adjustments to your sight
If you can't see that something is
Such as God's love and that you're His

Don't be discouraged. Be content
In spite of any trial sent
Since Christ arose after He died
Keep encouragement hidden inside

A Blessing

I often overestimate blessings in my thoughts
With the idea that one I must grab
Then it slips through my fingers very soon
When I see that I can't take the good with the bad

I must not think of what if it I lose
Because that means I'm thinking of days unarrived
Putting emphasis on it and not faith in God
And not on the way that thank God I've survived

There are imperfections with every blessing
So, I must see each moment individually
The times that mean change I must handle with wisdom
And I must praise the Lord for the good times He gives to me

When I realize I can take the good with the bad
When I take each moment one at a time
When I praise the Lord for each moment He gives
I can handle things wisely and stay in my prime

So one moment at a time, I enjoy this blessing
I don't worry if tomorrow it is or isn't here
I use it today and leave worry alone
It isn't my God and I must make that clear

Get Moving

Start to get into the frame
Of not acting like it's a game
Of not acting like you're just floating
But to things you're your mind devoting

Check things out and get on cue
Consider what's out there to do
And plan things out that slowly lead
To getting you the things you need

Yes, God does lots of the parts
But too, you've got to use your smarts
And everybody has to move
Their butts for God's pure parts to prove

Faith plus works go hand in hand
There's no fuss or firm demand
It's what you like and it's no bore
To do what you were put here for

So, go out and let God shine
Seek, inquire, stand in line
Be determined. Expect the best
And yes God, He will do the rest

Holy Spirit in Me

Holy Spirit, in me
Help me be all I am to be
And stay inside my heart, soul and mind
As the path that God has for me I try to find

God, please let Your Holy Spirit fill
My whole being, as I try doing Your will
Forgive all my sins and blot out my mistakes
With Your love and mercy since that's what it takes

Let the Holy Spirit increase and protect
Not be someone that I ignore or neglect
Let Him direct my steps and lighten my mood
Let Him fill me much better than any good food

With Your Holy Spirit, God I will proceed
It is who I want and who I always need
Just as Jesus has promised us, let it be so
Let the Holy Spirit dwell in me wherever I go

Don't Sit There and Expect the Worst

Don't sit there and expect the worst
Have some good sentences rehearsed
Of how things all will turn out right
Even if it's by faith not sight

Don't you know that God knows your name
"I will be blessed," you must proclaim
The future isn't very clear
But know that you should have no fear

God got you through things in the past
No bad moment in life will last
God will perfect you and provide
God's gonna help you out, decide

Never, ever at times recite
Verses of things not going right
Speak life and victory all day
Watch what you think. Watch what you say

Also, yourself don't condemn
If people strike, don't dwell on them
Speak positively and put God first
Don't sit there and expect the worst

God Doesn't Hate You

No, God doesn't hate you
Meditate on that a lot
He will get you all the way through
Any trouble you have got

God may see you trying
Feeling you can't do
Having, selling, buying
The way that you used to

And He looks upon
You when things you loose
Think of all He has done
And faithfulness still choose

Your life has meaning
But it's not defined
By how things are seeming
Keep God on your mind

God is on your side
And that is just great
You do not have to hide
For you God does not hate

Do Not Doubt Yourself

Do not doubt yourself any more
Learn from where that got you before
Look to Christ, gain strength and proceed
And know He is all that you need

Shivers may come and the way may be trying
But Christ says He loves you and he isn't lying
So, get up and shine and start anew
Each day go accomplish what you need to do

God makes a way even if there are flaws
For all who try to obey His laws
He doesn't want to see you struck
By what some people call bad luck

God shelters you, cares for you, wants you to rise
Satan, not Christ is the one who tells lies
So, put on your armor, hold on to your gear
Do not doubt yourself and don't have any fear

God Can Make a Way

God can make a way out of no way
Everything around you may say
That you can't win or arise
But look to God with open eyes

Think on how God helped the lowly
Sometimes quickly, sometimes slowly
When it seemed there was no chance
Praise God in the song and dance

For God opens doors and rescues
Even after He sometimes tests you
To see if you still call His name
God's the right answer, not the blame

Don't think God isn't surely making
Ways for you instead of just taking
Things from you that He'll return
God can make a way out of no way, you learn

God Still Has a Plan for You

God still has a plan for you
Despite what they think and do
Who oppose you, understand it
Even if it's underhanded

God has not given up on you
No matter who you're talking to
The nice, the not nice and the rest
God wants for you the very best

Your story isn't over yet
Don't get all worried or upset
Due to some things not being in place
You'll make it through it with God's grace

It doesn't seem that way right now
But soon you will be saying how
God got you through even once more
To better than you were before

I Love You, Lord

I love you, Lord
I'll show you by
Having joy
That doesn't die

I love you, Lord
I'll show you by
Not hating others
I'll more than try

I love you, Lord
I'll show you by
Embracing peace
And that's no lie

I love you, Lord
I'll show you by
Singing your praises
That reach the sky

I love you, Lord
I'll show you by
The way I act
And testify

o Weapon

No weapon formed against me shall prosper
Times can be rough but soon they'll get softer
Even though when I am down
Others may kick me so that I might frown

But I can really smile inside
Because God's face He doesn't hide
Even when false allies propose
To steal my joy, they can't, God knows

Block my blessings and proceed
To take away what I most need
To stop me since my feet will step on
It will not prosper against me, the weapon

Faith is the Key

What am I going to do now?
I'll make it through this, but how?
I'll survive but it may be trying
Someday I'm gonna stop crying

Out to God asking Him why
He will reveal a good plan, by and by
For my life and my purpose. His will
Is that I do all I can do then stand still

God makes a way in the brisk and the cold
God makes me courageous, successful and bold
God keeps me going until things are grand
Although sometimes I don't know what God has planned

Faith is the key and is my stay
I know that God will make a way
Instead of "Why me?" I'll be saying "Wow!"
Faith is the key and I'll keep the faith now

Don't Quit

Winners never quit
Quitters never win
Keep your candle lit
Don't ever give in

Winners never quit
Quitters never win
Just remember it
Seek God and don't sin

Winners never quit
Quitters never win
Do not simply sit
Stand up and begin

To sing God's praise
To show that God is good
To know that He makes ways
Not always understood

So, you can be a winner
Do not doubt this one bit
No quitter and no sinner
You'll win if you don't quit

Appreciation

Thank You, God in appreciation
For release from condemnation
For the great gift of Your covering
That keeps the past terrors from hovering

The aim of adversity now is blocked
The door to trespass and temptation is locked
That bad thought that tortured me no longer lurks
And You've proven the Word of God every time works

I am happy to live in a purified way
And I thank You for small blessings every day
I can now embrace new life without feeling lost
And You, God gave this to me with peace, at no cost

Now I do love You with all of my heart, soul and mind
And I trust Jesus Christ who is patient and kind
And I can love all Your children sisterly, brotherly
As you perfect me with compassion, motherly

God is Kind

God is kind, I found out
From my journeys all about
And it makes me feel fine
It's God's power. His not mine

Not just fragile or unstable
God is strong and God is able
To make ways and to sustain
He will one time and time again

God is gracious and filled with mercy
He'll reach down to where it's dirty
To rescue and to uplift
God is kind and that's a gift

God Can

When I feel I'm not up to par
That my sufficiency is far
That I cannot complete a plan
It's time to realize God can

When I feel like I'm getting lost
And confidence is nearly tossed
Reduced so low, in my insides
It's time to realize God guides

When I feel like I'm shocked and shaken
That foes are right and not mistaken
About me when they express views
It's time to realize God renews

When anything comes up or harms
Such as insults and lying charms
And I feel not equipped for this
It's time to realize God is

Wonderful

Loss of tasks, loss of things
Still Christ rides. Still Christ clings
Nothing changes what's in store
No more losses anymore

Can't see how this can be so
But somehow it's true I know
Overflowing riches wait
On a path that's clear and straight

Though it now seems rocky, winding
There's a future, bright I'm finding
The tunnel's dark but there's an end
That God controls and God will send

No longer loss and all to gain
No more attempts at causing pain
From enmity that becomes null
Someday things will be wonderful

For Your Good

Faith and action hand in hand
May not always understand
But keep pressing, idle not
Actions some and faith a lot

Do not dwell on what seems far
Do not dwell on how things are
Dwell on what must be within
In the heart, beneath the skin

Stressing can weigh quite a bit
Let it go. Let God have it
Can't control height or growth of hair
God can, so let go despair

May mean moving comfort zone
Never will mean left alone
Christ goes with you in it, yes
He can comfort. He can bless

Do what you must as you're led
Do get worries out of head
Do all that you must and should
God works all things out for your good

God's Got This

I'd try to grab all that I own
I'd try to go it all alone
I'd dwell on things that thieves can steal
I'd act as if Christ wasn't real

I'd do what I did with distress
I'd worry more instead of less
I'd try hard to myself defend
I'd act as if I had no friend

I prayed. God answered. Not assured
All that He gave, I'd try to hoard
He gently whispered, "I've got this"
I gave Him no handshake or kiss

When I my limited reached, to faint
Was all I could do and a saint
I felt far from until Christ said
"I'm still here for you. You're not dead"

I gave up all my own intent
To do God's will. With me Christ went
I'm never sure just how He will
But in the end, He's blessed me still

The Lord's in Charge

The Lord can do what others can't
His promise is not small or scant
His love beyond all measures rests
He'll take you on journeys and quests

His light shines. Never will it fade
He loves the temples that He made
He watches over, counsels, reigns
Over us each. He bears no stains

Someday, after we live life right
We too will shine in garments white
And share His glory in the skies
The soul that serves Him never dies

We all now brace for His return
He wants us to rise, not to burn
He wants us to for Him take stands
The Lord's in charge. We're in His hands

This Will All Become Clear

No matter what anyone says
No matter what anyone does
Jesus and God are on your side
Jesus and God always was

No matter if relationships sour
No matter what nastiness is revealed
Jesus and God are against the enemy
Jesus and God have you sealed

No matter how lowly
No matter how high
Jesus and God are with you
Jesus and God loves you is why

No matter about a tainted past
No matter about past deception
God and Jesus have all the power
Jesus, God's Son can mold to perfection

Jesus makes it better in the end
Jesus makes it easier to bear
He supplies all you need
This will all become clear

A Dim Night of Mourning

Anger sets in but first I deny
After floods of tears cleanse my soul, I sigh
Later with dry eyes, I inwardly cry
Then I start to accept it and stop asking why

It's a loss which at this time cannot be retrieved
A loss with a lesson on being bereaved
A loss I must live with but after I've grieved
After the initial pain is relieved

Him I have to let go I was blessed to receive
Yet it never occurred to me one day he'd leave
My wrist becomes moist as my tears wet my sleeve
Please give me some time. Let me grieve on this eve

Time will stand still till the sun starts to set
I can't interact. I'm not over this yet
Right now it's not hard to forgive and forget
How I wish that I'd hugged him the last time we met

For tonight I will dwell in a shell like a clam
Faced with some test of faith for which I couldn't cram
But I know I will be alright in the AM
When I start seeing the light of the Lamb

Like a blanket of comfort, the Son's light I seek
Creeps in on the horizon as prophets speak
Slowly grief tapers off and faith starts to peak
Intense pain gets eased and hope strengthens the weak

"Life will be given to those that are dead
Joy will replace every tear that is shed
We will watch as the ones who now sleep go ahead
Before each loss becomes a reunion instead."

God is quite awesome. The pain He has cured
By the blood of the Lamb, I am now reassured
That inside of His mansion our seats are secured
On a dim night of mourning, faith grew and matured

God Blesses Body, Mind and Soul

God blesses body, mind and soul
Makes prosper, sturdy, has control
Assures, establishes and reigns
And never makes losses without gains

For anything that's snatched away
For being too blind to obey
God gently turns and God corrects
And gives back more than one expects

One may spend days chastised for sin
But God will sure let one back in
And open doors that seemed locked
With God no good thing will be blocked

So take what God, the Father dishes
For He lets take place what He wishes
Someday, somehow, He'll lift His hand
And reveal wonders He has planned

God will show you how you can rise
In ways you'd never realize
So hold on tight and pray and trust
Because God loves you and you must

What God Has for You You'll Get

What God has for you you'll get
You will be all satisfied and set
You will be overjoyed throughout
You will see what He's talking about

What presents to open for you to obtain
Will be gotten by you and will still remain
You can use some and save some
For His members He put some away and He gave some

What God makes life's pattern consist of
How He observes, helps and stands in the midst of
Your obedience journey and your ever trying
Will make you see God's face without denying

What God settles in you you'll appreciate
All His goodness He'll show off and will demonstrate
All He wants to show you, all great and higher
What God wills to do for you should inspire

God Can Bless Even a Mess

Patterns of things out of place
Movement of things to an unideal place
Environment unstable, causing high levels of stress
God can bless even a mess

Climate uncomfortable and lots of rain
Circumstances such as can drain
All kinds of issues to address
God can bless even a mess

Situations and issues with bills
Concerns and worries such as can cause chills
Moving on nonetheless
God can bless even a mess

God can make you closer to Him
He can fill your cup of joy to the brim
God can teach you faith and faithfulness
God can bless even a mess

The Lord Will Supply

When you're in trouble like unseen
When something not right has you bound
Still know you are a king or queen
Still praise the Lord and stick around

When you ask God how long it's lasting
God hasn't turned a deaf ear
Keep going, obeying, praying, fasting
The Lord wants you to know that He is always near

When you are in a dreadful bind
When you see no way out
God has surprises, the best kind
God's always with you so have no doubt

When you ask God for the right time to proceed
When you want to get what you lack
The Lord will supply your every need
And on you He won't turn His back

The Rescue

God is strength, power and might
He makes everything turn out right
God is merciful and pure
In God's hands you can be secure

God is help and in the lead
God is everything you need
God is inside of the people you see
God frustrates and beats Satan valiantly

God is all glory in
God purges all repented-for sin
God has for His children royal attire
It's white though some used to be sows in the mire

God purified you, don't forget
The devil is His little pet
The devil backs off when God says to
God then moves in for the rescue

On Jesus Call

If you are ever lost
If you are ever tempest tossed
If you are ever in despair
Call on Jesus. He is there

If you ever can't grin
If you are riddled with dark sin
If you feel really downed
Call on Jesus and He'll come around

If you ever feel very confused
If you ever feel unexcused
If you ever feel that your light isn't lit
Call on Jesus whose love doesn't quit

If you feel you can't make it through
If you need inspiration in the things you do
If anything goes wrong at all
Call on Jesus. On Jesus call

God Fixes It

Everything that happens to you God fixes it
When there is a mix up, God also un-mixes it
Don't worry for a minute, for God is for you
He would never despise, mock or ignore

God aims to build you up, strengthen you too
Turn your back on and don't see the old. See the new
Pick up your cross, have joy but deny yourself
Christ will be with you and you won't be by yourself

It might be pitch dark now but it will be light
Christ can make all things lovely so walk upright
His Word teaches you how to powerfully go on
And He can fill you up with His Spirit to grow on

The road still may get rocky but God embraces you
In refreshing and in restful places God places
Now to the Lord above you can forever go
Working on you is His pleasure. He won't let you go

A Journey to Faith
and Praise

Sometimes darkness seems to cover
But it can be like just an illusion
It's all only for you to discover
Your Master, Jesus', intrusion

Sometimes things need to be figured out
Sometimes the solution is simple but hidden
But just one explanation is all it's about
Letting it keep you down is forbidden

Sometimes some monster seeks to invade
But Jesus must commission a chase
Christ causes the threatening image to fade
And can make it run off as if in a race

In the end peace, goodness and health are restored
In the end the words Victory and Peace resound
And the enemy's ploy gets completely ignored
Praise God up above. He's the best cure you've found

Rose Before, This Time I Will

I felt down like from a hard fall
As if I had nothing left at all
As if I'd tumbled off a hill
I rose before. This time I will

I felt emptied of what I had
I felt pretty worried and pretty bad
I could not even pay a bill
I rose before. This time I will

Seemed all of my troubles suddenly came
I started to feel guilt and shame
But soon my goals God did fulfill
I rose before. This time I will

I'll just describe it as a spell
I know the Lord's potency well
I'll wait on Him and I'll be still
I rose before. This time I will

onetheless

Do what you don't feel like doing
Go where you don't feel like going
Override your doubt with action
Your turned-off with satisfaction

Get the feel of a new environment
Come out of your dull retirement
That is in your state of thought
Think. Be thought of. Teach. Be taught

Get out of your comfort zone
With God on your side, you are never alone
He can work through you if you just arise
And flee negative thinking with all of its ties

Set your sights on impossible goals
Think of the Lord who provides and consoles
Think of what you can be if your actions permit
Then do all of the things that will lead up to it

Sure, you may feel like it doesn't matter
But good things don't come on a silver platter
Sometimes discouragement tries to hinder success
But you must take the right steps, nonetheless

To Know My God

I'm so blest to know my God
I've had my share of my "Why God?"
Something always brings Him back, it's never "Goodbye God"
Because He is a merciful, caring and high God

I hate that I went off and grieved God
When I came clean, it all relieved God
He chastised me, then I believed God
Hope I never fall again, since I've received God

Now I can clearly live and enjoy God
I hope not again to do things that annoy God
If I have any trouble, I'll simply employ God
I now have God forever and none can destroy God

I live life God's way with light that's from God
He's filled with compassion. He isn't a numb God
He's a when you need Him, call and He'll come God
He's a make you feel happy, sing, dance and hum God

To Being Obedient, Solid and Firm

Prejudice, mocking, violence, beating
Staring, mistaking, mislabeling, cheating
Impoliteness peaking, not speaking
No sense. Apparent weakling

Rude outbursts, cussing, litter
Nasty looks, acting bitter
Stealing, complaining, wrong places remaining
No sense. None claiming

Approaching with ill intent
Misrepresenting what we represent
No regard, trying hard
No sense. Off guard

Talking of ones in adverse ways
Not caring if they hear what you say
Making fun, more than one
No sense. Already done

Why we do what we do can't always be cleared
But we can change afterwards when God is feared
To being obedient, solid and firm
Because Christ's help is there always, not just short-term

Faith, Hope and Love

I locked myself indoors and got on my knees
Asking, "What must I do, my Lord to please?"
I decided to give all my goods to the poor
"But, said my Lord, I need something more."

I decided with faith to be mainly concerned
Then on possibly giving my body to be burned
Then on understanding all knowledge and mysteries
"But," said my Lord, It's not about these."

I decided to pray that with tongues I would speak
Tongues of men and of angels. That gift I'd seek
And my pleasing my Savior would then come to pass
"But, said my Lord, Tinkling symbals, sounding brass."

So, I went out and sought around persons and crowds
"I will find what I'm searching" for is what I vowed
There were rules to which some of them didn't adhere
And I'd wish they'd face punishment, very severe

And when selfishness on their part was shown
I would say to myself, "I too seek my own."
There was lying and sin and about it I joked
Plus, I thought evil and was easily provoked

But once all this disturbed me, I thought of those nails
And I heard my Lord saying that love never fails
And although as a child I had acted and spake
I now do know what pleasing my Lord will take

Now, I want for others what is right and good
And all of my Lord's answers are now understood
I am to have faith, hope and love, not hate
Love being the one that is surely most great

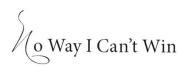o Way I Can't Win

God blesses in the night
God blesses in the light
Although there are stresses
God blesses

Seemingly, I was blank
Trouble full at highest rank
Now they are gone. My soul is eased
I'm grateful not displeased

The outlook for me was simply black
I died inside but I came back
Now I walk in the day, not blind
I leave the darkness behind

I look at the old as a daze
I focus now on better ways
Awakened now, sometimes I still fail
God helps me fight, though, tooth and nail

I pull the covers from atop my head
I stand and move and forget the bed
In all that I do. If I stood, if I tripped
My Lord now keeps me well equipped

I'm looking forward to years, long
Determined and positive, wise and strong
Despite ups and downs and each out and in
There's no way I can't win

Can't See Beyond

Beyond this life that's temporary
Visions obstructed for reasons that vary
Reasons, excuses, they're all the same
Need sometimes, greed sometimes, sometimes blame

Beyond this world and worldly treasures
Worldly possessions, worldly pleasures
To recognize the best of two bosses
One ensures gains. One guarantees losses

Beyond needs which would still be provided
To realize that you are sadly misguided
Someday you'll die. This is serious
Know that God's ways are mysterious

Seek, choose Jesus. Get a Bible to read
He will provide your every need
Treasures in heaven are never-ending
Please take heed. Your ways need mending

Can't see beyond serving to kill
Quit Satan's work and serve God's will
This is His calling and if you respond
You can look past what you can't see beyond

The Wooded Hill

As I walked up that wooded hill
Afraid of heights, I did it still
Until I learned every rule
Not to fall down and feel like a fool

The first rule is to never look back
You must keep looking forward to stay on track
You must not hold onto the things that were lost
You mustn't look back, at any cost

The second rule is to watch out for rocks
They can knock off your shoes and rip off your socks
But worst of all, they can ruin your trip
If you don't watch for rocks, they may cause you to slip

The third rule is to take your time
You have to be patient throughout your climb
You'll reach the top when the time is right
Don't be impatient. It makes you uptight

The next rule is to be positive
To give that climb all you can give
To know you're gonna reach the top
Until you do, you never stop

Finally but not least, having faith and trust
In Jesus' love for you is a must
And know He walks right by your side
You cannot go wrong when God is your guide

Trust In the Lord

Seems circumstances are out to get me
Right now, I'm not quite sure what hit me
I feel frustrated, alone and bored
There's one thing I need now: Trust in the Lord

Seems no one else is on my side
I've lost my friends. I've lost my pride
I only wish to save my soul
To trust in the Lord becomes my goal

My world seems empty with no true possession
I felt I was punished. I learned of Jesus' intercession
And after that, I felt I must
Turn to the Lord and place my trust

The tears I cry are so profuse
I struggle daily through lots of abuse
I felt as though it was a curse
I'll trust in the Lord now through better or worse

Sometimes I feel I want to quit
There's something I must not forget
If I just keep going, there'll be a reward
I always must trust in the Lord

ake This Exchange

Your enemy, the one who fights you
Disrespects you, hates you, spites you
Tries to bring you down, down low
Even one you call a foe

You must also love and pray for
Throw all foolish pride away for
This isn't stupid, far-fetched or strange
If you know Christ, you can make this exchange

A child of God has a blest job
The devil is out to kill, destroy, rob
To snatch away your root and stem
Take Christ from you so that you'll act like them

Rather than that, you must choose to share
God's love is great and there's much to spare
Don't let them rob you. Share instead
Love even enemies, just as Christ did

I Have the Lord

I have all I'll ever need
Did not have to beg and plead
Don't own a house or decent car
My friends? I don't know where they are

I have no gold or diamond ring
Don't own one expensive thing
Struggled so and lost a lot
But all I'll ever need, I've got

The hardships that I face are tough
But what I have is quite enough
For comfort when the world gets colder
I just lean on the dear Lord's shoulder

I feel down and ashamed no more
Though some may say I'm very poor
I feel I'm rich. I feel fulfilled
I have the Lord and I am thrilled

A Better Life

Many folks are questioning
Why there's so much suffering
Why some problems hit so hard
Which we can't simply disregard

And we may become upset
But we mustn't give up yet
There is someone on which to lean
And a life that's yet unseen

When one lives to serve God's will
Life, perhaps, seems trying still
This is something we now face
But there will be another place

It's a lovely path to follow
In this place, there'll be no sorrow
There will be joy and love and peace
A new life that will never cease

We've still got time to prepare
In hopes to someday make it there
In hopes we'll all suffer no more
A better life is what's in store!

Forgive Us Our Sins

There are times when I've done others wrong
When I've done things that I shouldn't do
When I weakened but should have been strong
Lord, my sins aren't hidden from you

There are others who made me feel hurt
There are those by whom I've been mistreated
They put me down, treat me like dirt
And have lied, stolen, gossiped and cheated

I don't need to be overly worried
About all that others have done
For my burdens, you Lord have carried
And in your eyes, we all are as one

So, I ask that you make our hearts true
Give us all bread and fruit of the vine
That all our sins be forgiven by you
Not only the ones that are mine

Faith Is

The strength and endurance that I request
The thinking that keeps my mind at rest
When nothing else seems comforting, quietly
Faith comes in and covers a variety

For the threat of Satan's clever snares
For the lengthy struggle that no one shares
For the times when obeying Christ seems strange
Faith surely handles a very wide range

Alternative to all sorts of addictions
Management of all sorts of afflictions
Loneliness, anger, depression…and grief
Faith offers healing and causes relief

It has such power, I have found
It loosened chains by which I was bound
Could be the ten-thousandth trial or the eighth
There's nothing defeating as long as there's faith

Growing From the Soil

Growing from the soil
In summer, it was dry
Sometimes I had to toil
Sometimes I'd stop and cry

The loneliest of all
In Autumn I felt sorrow
I watched each petal fall
I waited for tomorrow

In the wintertime
Life was mostly cold
I stood beneath the rime
No petals to unfold

Springtime has began
I'm growing more and more
While following God's plan
This day long waited for

Jesus, I receive you
Forsaking my self-will
More clearly I perceive you
Now life is such a thrill

God I'll always serve!
God I'll always praise!
All praises You deserve
You bring me through each phase

Thou Art Loosed

The strength she had had not been firm
And this condition was long-term
Upon her back, the plowers plowed
And for this reason, she was bowed

She'd been this way for years, eighteen
This weakened state was not unseen
It drew attention from the crowd
Infirmity, it had her bowed

Her spirit had been very poor
Her eyes could only see the floor
For evil forces took effect
This woman couldn't stand erect

When she still sought Him, Jesus saw
Regardless of the Sabbath law
That hypocrites and leaders used
The Master told her, "Thou art loosed."

At once, this woman stood up straight
And now set free, she didn't wait
Yes, God this woman glorified
Thou art loosed, woman! Do not hide

Prayer is Just a Whisper Away

Close your eyes and take a breath
Resuscitate your spirit's death
Determine what you need to say
Prayer is just a whisper away

When you need to make a choice
He doesn't need to hear your voice
Talking inwardly is okay
Prayer is just a whisper away

When you're tempted, even a lot
You can receive help on the spot
Escape from sin, the strength to obey
Prayer is just a whisper away

When there are pressures, stressors, pain
The instinct may be to complain
But it is best to simply pray
Prayer is just a whisper away

To Never Be Alone

If I found out how it would be to never be alone
I'd find there's someone close to me that I can call my own
That someone watches over me of whom I am a part
And that would fill the vacancy that's deep within my heart

Some say that angels guard us all throughout the day and night
I pray that God who I can call on when I'm not alright
Will send by His commands when I'm in trouble or alone
Some of His helping hands, so I won't trip upon a stone

It's faith and strength I seek to make my spirit clean and pure
To grow as does a seed and shield the pains that I'll endure
If I believe and feel inside that someone else is there
That comfort, then, would be my guide in times of deep despair

So many times I weaken when God puts me to the test
If I get what I seek, then He can put my mind to rest
By helping me to see it's true. The Lord is by my side
And those He sends to guard me too and light to be my guide

And so He has and now indeed, I see and trust and know
The Holy Spirit plants the seed where faith and strength will grow
I'm not alone when no one's there to see or hear or touch
Therefore, no evil do I fear. God loves us very much

Fallen Short in Any Way?

Fallen short in any way?
Disobeyed on any day?
Realize and understand
That you've gone against the least command?

Felt you weren't obligated
To avoid the sin you demonstrated?
That imperfection is a cause
For not detesting sinful flaws?

We are not blemish-less by far
And oh, how wretched we all are
Yes imperfection is a fact
But not finding comfort in any wrong act

Perfection has to be our aim
Accepting sin must cause us shame
We serve the law of God in the mind
When we try to forsake sin, every kind

And the key is to really try
Yes, wretched ones are you and I
But when the flesh we mind not
It is as if we have no spot

This is since Jesus demonstrated
That all wrong-doing should be hated
And taught commands, specifically
That help us out terrifically

We really must try to obey
And believe sin is not okay
And if we truly hate all sin
The Spirit, not our flesh will win

And we'll become perfected, yes
When Christ comes to reward and bless
Will that your sins amount to none
In order to conquer, like Jesus the Son

I Shall Escape

Right now, I dwell in solitude
And negative is how that's viewed
It makes me feel so strange and weird
I told myself that no one cared

Right now, where could a good job be?
And what would be an enjoyable hobby?
This is no comforting or friendly place
But with patience, I'll see the Lord's face

How these times give me restless rest
But they're a contest and a test
Over so many divers tricks
I win when no-no good thought sticks

No angry or destructive mind frame will I keep
I won't be a glutton for food, drinks or sleep
No drug abuse. No way, form, or shape
Soliciting sinners, I shall escape

Even if in the past I've failed
This time, obedience will be nailed
I shall escape the fowler's snare
With God's own help. Yes, Christ does care

Replaced With a Blessing

For the gifts of God to be obtained
Mourning ceased and comfort gained
Hunger and thirst for righteousness filled
Strength and endurance must be instilled

To receive mercy, merciful be
Be pure in heart and God you will see
A peacemaker is called God's daughter or son
By the poor in spirit, the Kingdom is won

Those that are meek will be like queens and kings
Inherit the earth, wonderful things
Those persecuted for righteousness' sake
The Kingdom of Heaven is theirs too, to take

Those suffering for Christ's sake, rejoice
Strength and endurance, a wise choice
Just as the prophets' of times past
Your reward in heaven is vast

Blessed are they said Jesus, blest
For with them each God is pleased and impressed
Be reassured that what now seems depressing
Will be forgotten, replaced with a blessing

When I'm Falling

Things seem to all come apart
Just when I've decided
To keep the Lord inside my heart
And not to be misguided

When I say that my strength is built
That I will not turn back
I end up feeling down with guilt
And on the same wrong track

After I just feel so sure
That I've got myself together
I then become so insecure
Then comes the stormy weather

Sometimes I feel like such a mess
Could I, too have a calling?
I asked the Lord and He said "Yes,
I catch you when you're falling."

I think of this when I start to fall
When I just feel like crying
The Lord will get me through this all
I'm gonna keep on trying

A Far Worse Fate

Some misfortune sure can strike
Faced with things we do not like
Even those, we can appreciative
If we learn to block a far worse state

Not retaliation's wish
But the dirt that ones can dish
Is not causing me to hate
But to hope they dodge a far worse fate

Would not ask that my enemy
Would suffer so unpleasantly
But would repent, before too late
And be shielded from a far worse fate

Some are said to have such luck
As their sins they hide and tuck
Still, it's better not to wait
But to warn them of a far worse fate

Or they'll regret every offense
There will be pain that's so intense
That you now can't calculate
For the ones who choose a far worse fate

Give God Praise

Give God praise for awaking you
Praise Him for making you
Praise for your oxygen
Praise for forgiving sin

For the path Jesus paved
And every soul He saved
Suffering so immensely
Praise God sincerely, intensely

Praise Him for sunshine, trees
Standing or on your knees
Praise God for every flower
God, only, has all power

Praise God in any case
No matter what you face
Praise God in bad times too
You'll find He'll comfort you

Glory to God, Amen!
For He accepts us when
We leave our sinful ways
God is great! Give Him praise

$\mathcal{A}$cknowledgements

This book was inspired by well many well-known authors such as Joel Osteen, Joyce Meyer, T.D. Jakes and others, including Matt Damon, Susan L. Taylor and by the written and spoken word of Jesus Christ. It was a pleasure for me to read and to continue reading various inspirational, motivational and educational books and to glean treasures that help, motivate and inspire me in such that the benefits last a lifetime.

I thank all of the authors of the writings I've read, little-known, well-known and unknown. I also thank Jesus Christ, God the Father and all of my readers.

About the Author

Michelle Marie Richardson has been working as a Respiratory Therapist for over 21 years and has been writing poetry since childhood. She is publishing this book because she wants to help encourage others with her Christ-centered poetry which she uses to encourage herself, also, along with the Bible and a personal relationship with Jesus who has helped her in hard times and through many trials. Michelle has read and reads many positive books and writings which help to inspire her poetry, as well.

Printed in the United States
By Bookmasters